JOEL EDWARDS

Falling back on God

A Lent group study on trust

kevin mayhew

First published in 2005 by

KEVIN MAYHEW LTD
Buxhall, Stowmarket, Suffolk, IP14 3BW
E-mail: info@kevinmayhewltd.com
Web: www.kevinmayhew.com

Scripture quotations are from the *Holy Bible, New International
Version*, copyright © 1973, 1978, 1984 by International Bible
Society. Used by permission of Hodder & Stoughton, a
member of the Hodder Headline Group.

9 8 7 6 5 4 3 2 1 0

ISBN 1 84417 486 7
Catalogue No 1500856

Cover design by Jonathan Stroulger
Typesetting by Richard Weaver

Printed in Great Britain

Contents

About Joel Edwards

Revd Joel Edwards is the General Director of the Evangelical Alliance UK. His appointment was a historic event as the first black director in the Alliance's 150-year history. In June 2001 he was appointed as one of the first Honorary Canons of St Paul's Cathedral. Joel's vision is to see the Church become a movement for change, working together to bring biblical transformation to society.

Joel was born in Jamaica and came to Britain at the age of eight. He is married to Carol and has two grown-up children. He was a probation officer for ten years and former General Secretary of the African and Caribbean Evangelical Alliance. He is also an ordained minister of the New Testament Church of God and served as a member of its executive council for six years and as a local pastor for ten years.

Revd Edwards' ministry has drawn on his experience as a professional counsellor and involves a range of community-focused activities, including membership of the Home Office's Faith and Government Consultation Steering Group and the Home Secretary's National Policing Forum.

Joel works extensively in the press and media. His television and radio appearances include BBC1's *Question Time* and such Radio 4 programmes as *The Moral Maze* and *Any Questions*. He is a regular contributor to *Thought for the Day* and *The Daily Service*.

His first book, *Lord Make Us One – But Not All The Same!* was published in February 1999 and is a semi-autobiographical work which presents his own pilgrimage as an object lesson in contemporary evangelical diversity in the UK. *The Cradle, the Cross and the Empty Tomb* first appeared in December 2000, and his third book *Hope, Respect and Trust – Valuing These Three* was published in September 2004.

Introduction

Imagine a society in which no one trusts each other. A world in which every child under 18 is electronically monitored by their parent or guardian and in which every passenger scrutinises the credentials of the pilot before they board the plane. Horrendous!

Trust is a social and community glue. Without it, as the poet W. B. Yeats suggests, 'things fall apart, the centre cannot hold'. But it's more than that. Trust is the passport by which we are given permission to enter other people's worlds in order to give and receive of ourselves. 'The shared social life of free persons is a densely woven fabric of promise keeping', said Jurgen Moltmann, 'and it cannot exist without trust'. Trust is therefore a profoundly spiritual thing. It is what it means to be a person. God made us to be trusting and asks us to be trustworthy.

Ultimately, Christian faith is rooted in a trust-worthy God. No one else comes near. This is what the Psalmist means by his refusal to trust in princes or other mortals (Psalm 146:3). But it is from this secure environment that we experiment with all other trusting relationships. This kind of trust/faith saves us from the suffocation of cynicism.

Cynicism has never been a mark of abundant life, for cynicism is a feather shield against the possibility of pain: and only dead people feel no pain. By contrast, the living learn to trust, because they have learned to lean on God. Trust is therefore a mirror image of faith. Like faith it demands relationships and cries out for interaction with *A. N. Other*. On its own it makes no sense: in isolation it is useless. To trust is to be conscious of other people as we blend their vulnerability with our own.

God knows our world is impossible without this kind of trusting faith. This is why he has called and commissioned us.

And God has a right to do so because in spite of our weaknesses, he has a habit of trusting us. He trusted Moses, the Patriarchs and the prophets. He entrusted Jesus to a teenage virgin and her fiancé. Peter, James, Paul and Timothy were all trusted. So are you.

That's why this Lent study will focus on trust. The Psalms have so much to say on this important issue of trust, and so our study will take us through five themes with readings from the Psalms. The key passages are printed and portions of the text have been underlined; these will be explored further in the notes. It would be good for you to read the entire psalm to get the wider context of the brief texts. There are also some points for personal application and a meditation based on the theme. The study's *Talk time* is your opportunity to discuss some of the key points arising from the material. And finally there is a *To do* list – a kind of takeaway meal which should help to earth the things you have learned and prayed through.

The study is aimed at helping small groups focus on God's Word during Lent, but it should also serve you well if for any reason you prefer to study on your own.

Week 1
When Foundations Give Way

When <u>the foundations are being destroyed</u>,
  what can the righteous do?
<u>The Lord is in his holy temple;</u>
  <u>the Lord is on his heavenly throne</u>.
He observes the sons of men;
  his eyes examine them.

Psalm 11:3,4

Reflections from the Psalm

I have only ever been in an earth tremor once in my life. It happened in Jamaica when I was about 7 years old. I can still remember the awful sensation of the earth rumbling underneath me and the feeling that there was nothing else to do but wait for something really bad *not* to happen.

The picture painted by the psalmist is one of moral and social upheaval. Whatever the foundations were we cannot mistake the impression that things in the social order were giving way and 'the foundations of law and order have collapsed' (New Living Translation). Any number of incidents in David's life might mark the point at which this was taking place. It might have been the trauma of a despotic and demonised King Saul chasing him across the desert, the incestuous behaviour of his son Amnon, or Absalom's insurrection. In any of those cases – and many more besides, David may well have experienced the earth shaking and the foundations giving way. Indeed, if you cannot trust a king to whom you have pledged loyalty, or your own son not to lead an army against you, then who can you trust?

David's response was based on his sense of trust in God. And this trust was based on two important facts. First, God was in his temple. He was still David's object of worship. What defined the nation as the people of God was the worship of Yahweh and nothing else embodied this identity as much as the tabernacle and temple. The temple was therefore the place for personal piety and corporate identity, and God was still in charge of it. This was his reference point of stability. When David's foundations gave way, God in his holy temple remained his moral compass.

But he also remembered that God was on his heavenly throne. If a general talks about another general it has a certain weight attached to it. That's simply because he knows what he is talking about! Perhaps no other king has ever spoken as much of God as King as David did. David really understood the weight of the illustration. To say that God is on his throne is to make him sovereign over civic affairs as much as over personal devotion. God as King cannot be brushed into the margins of private piety. Directly or indirectly, God watches over and examines people's behaviour. He knows what's going on and will go to any lengths to execute justice. This kind of God can be trusted, therefore, even when foundations give way.

A moment's meditation

> Because he lives I can face tomorrow;
> because he lives all fear is gone;
> because I know he holds the future,
> and life is worth the living
> just because he lives.

A personal application

In the 2003 Reith Lectures, Onora O'Neil dealt extensively with the subject of trust. In her lectures she suggested that in many ways people today are no less trusting than they once were. The difference, she suggests, is that our influential media have created more high profile stories of mistrust, leaving us with the impression that there is a lot less trust about. There is no doubting the strength of her argument; our modern media have a lot to answer for in this regard. But imaginary or otherwise, today's world wrestles with a real crisis of trust. Many people feel that the foundations are giving way. A society whose growing disbelief has been signalled by emblems of mistrust is showing real signs of brokenness.

As we approach Lent we must recognise that we too are a part of that brokenness. It is being measured by the upward spiralling of crime and social disorder, families being pulled apart and the challenge to community cohesion. As I write these notes, Britain is still reeling from the tragedy of our first British-born suicide bombers in London.

Like David, we too must recognise God as being in his holy temple. We must fix trusting eyes upon him.

If you have ever wondered how a gymnast or ice skater keep their balance whilst spinning at great speed, the answer is fairly basic. They learn to keep their eyes on a fixed point in the building. The key is to keep your eyes on God. He is the God who is ever faithful. From his holy temple he watches over us in order both to guide and protect. When in our personal tragedies, mistakes or loss, foundations give way, we can know what it means to stand in sinking sand. If things give way around us, it is all too easy to avert our gaze from God.

But God isn't in the temple alone: he is on his throne and it is in our corporate and personal relationship with God that we renew our vision of events in the world. People who really look at God should know best what he is able to do when things fall apart.

And we know this because we also remember that judgement ultimately belongs to God. Suicide bombers 'and those who love violence' have already been reckoned with. Our King of righteousness who loves justice sits in G8 Summits and keeps accounts of corruption. While we pray in his temple we also work in his world because we trust his judgement in world affairs as readily as we trust his inscrutable dealings in our lives.

A prayer

O Lord,
    when our foundations are shaken
    and nothing we hold holds firm,
    we put our trust in you.
In our shared despair
    and fractured hopes
    we put our trust in you.

We worship at your temple,
    and as we meet you there,
    restore and renew our love;
    open our hearts and minds.

You know everything about us;
    tell us something more about you.

We kneel at your throne
    and bow down.
When we are overwhelmed,
    remind us you are the King
    of all peoples.
In our broken homes,
    you reign.
In the places of power and influence,
    you reign.
In our palaces and on our pavements,
    you reign.
For you are everybody's God.

O Lord,
    when nothing we hold holds firm,
    we put our trust in you.

Talk time

- If Christ is in his 'holy temple' what difference will this make to your devotional life and your ability to trust him in your private devotion?

- If God really is 'on his heavenly throne' how much do we reflect that in our prayers? Watch the news this week from the perspective of God being in control and see what difference it makes to your prayers.

To do

- As Lent reminds us of Christ's Passion, make a list of the sufferings of our world.

- Can you recall the last incident in which you really trusted God in prayer and emerged with a real testimony of his response to that trust?

Week 2
Falling Backwards on God

Trust in the Lord and do good;
dwell in the land and enjoy safe pasture.
Delight yourself in the Lord
and he will give you the desires of your heart.

Commit your way to the Lord;
trust in him and he will do this:
He will make your righteousness shine like the dawn,
the justice of your cause like the noonday sun.

Be still before the Lord and wait patiently for him;
do not fret when men succeed in their ways,
when they carry out their wicked schemes.

Psalm 37:3-7

Reflections from the Psalm

My daughter has never forgotten the times I used her as a visual aid for my sermons. In a sermon about trust I asked her to fall backwards and allow me to catch her. The idea was to let her fall further and further towards the floor before catching her, demonstrating just how far she was prepared to go before panicking. She fell pretty low (so to speak!) before we stopped the exercise. But at the age of 10 she was easy to catch. The trust count may not be as impressive with 15 stone colleagues in the trust-building seminars!

Through spiritual instinct and personal experience, the psalmist learned a lot about falling backwards on God. As a result he crams two ideas in the same breath: people who trust in God are in a good place to do good. And so we should. Putting yourself out for others can be as precarious as standing on a cliff edge but this girdle of confidence gives believers the safety to scale the heights of good deeds. Insecure Christians are too self-obsessed to think about doing good. They are usually too busy surviving in the world.

So for the psalmist, trusting in God was added value for living – not a crutch to survive by. 'Delight' and 'desire' are a part of his vocabulary. And his advice is that we commit our ways to God. In fact, it's more than a mental agreement to sign up with God: it's more like a lifestyle decision to throw oneself at God. It's falling backwards at 100 miles per hour!

David learned from experience that God was always dependable. Even when his personal righteousness was being questioned and when his own just cause was at stake he was able to 'be still'; quietly trusting as he fell backwards on God.

A moment's meditation

> *Lead us from death to life,*
> *from falsehood to truth.*
> *Lead us from despair to hope,*
> *from fear to trust.*
> *Lead us from hate to love,*
> *from war to peace.*
> *Let peace fill our heart,*
> *our world, our universe.*
>
> *Anglican Church of Aotearoa*

A personal application

During a visit to Zimbabwe some years ago I was walking past a funeral parlour when their advertising slogan caught my attention. It said, 'We're the last ones to let you down!'.

It's impossible to read the Psalms without feeling that God stands behind us saying, 'Go on, fall back. Trust me. I'll be the very last person to let you down'.

It's only as we discover and recover this sense of confidence in God that we begin to find the scope to hold others up. If you are paranoid about what others are thinking about you, or insecure about your prevailing circumstances, you are unlikely to find yourself, in the words of the psalmist, 'doing good'. And you certainly won't equate your faith with words such as 'enjoy' 'delight' or 'desire'. You are probably more inclined to talk about 'coping' and 'survival'.

Trust gives us the right social posture – even when things are positively not going our way. And it does so even when our credibility is at stake. All of us have those times when our reputation is on the line and we have become victims of misdemeanour or misunderstanding. Trust assures you that God will vindicate you: that sooner or later – dawn or midday – your just cause will become evident to everyone else.

And trust's best advice is to be still. Be still in the domestic dispute or in the office wrangling. And even if it becomes necessary to take legal action against the company, be still.

For stillness is falling backwards on a God who always pushes us upright again.

A prayer

Lord,
teach us to trust –
not in our skills or past achievements,
not in our reputations
    or renown.
Teach us to fall on you.

Teach us to trust
when we are mistaken and misheard,
misrepresented
    or misunderstood.
Teach us to fall on you.

Teach us to serve –
   to love the joy of giving;
not because we are repaid
   or praised.
But because you gave us first.

Teach us to let you work
   on our behalf.
Teach when we are right
   or wrong
to trust your vindicating love
and learn to fall on you.

For Jesus' sake.
Amen.

Talk time

- It's fine to talk about trusting and doing good but how do we help good people who trust and do good, only to find that bad things keep happening to them?

To do

- Try to measure the level of trust you exercise in God. How far are you willing to fall back on God? Here is a realistic way of doing this. Take a blank sheet of paper. On the left side make a list of real-life challenges which have faced you over the past six months. Now make a note on the right-hand side how much you felt you prayed through each issue, giving yourself an honest mark out of ten.

- If it's true that trusting people can help other people, how far has this been true in your life? Can you think of people you have reached out to in the past week?

- If you are an insecure Christian, is there someone you can talk with about this? Why not use the next six days to decide who you might talk with?

- Use the time now to be still and reflect on the things you have learned and the things you need to do.

Week 3
Confidence on a Cross

My God, my God, <u>why have you forsaken me?</u>
Why are you so far from saving me,
so far from the words of my groaning?
O my God, I cry out by day, but <u>you do not answer,</u>
by night, and am not silent.

<u>Yet you are enthroned</u> as the Holy One;
you are the praise of Israel.
<u>In you our fathers put their trust;</u>
they trusted and you delivered them.
<u>They cried to you and were saved;</u>
in you they trusted and were not disappointed.

Psalm 22:1-5

Reflections from the Psalm

I used to see signs in shops which said, 'In God we trust – everybody else pays cash!' It was a nice way of making the point even if the shopkeepers didn't actually believe in God.

Many people still believe in God today. In Britain at least 70 per cent of the population still believe in 'God'. That makes God more popular than any politician. The problem is that belief in God becomes a huge burden when he doesn't appear to take us as seriously as we take him.

That was David's problem. Perhaps no other psalm begins as poignantly as this psalm. David is utterly confused by what appears to be God's abandonment. It was hard for David to deal with God's silence, for silence usually feels like another name for rejection. As C. S. Lewis once noted, we can cope with God saying 'yes' or 'no', but it's his silence which shakes our trust most severely.

'Yet' is a very big word. It makes all the difference that God remains supreme. In other words, God is greater than David's feelings of rejection. And what is more, God has a track record of faithfulness going back to the Patriarchs, and David remembered that those who put their faith in this God were never embarrassed. Within a few verses, therefore, David journeys from despair to hope.

On the cross Jesus made a very similar journey. Bible scholars and preachers have said a great deal about the last words of Jesus on the cross. What is important to us in this study is to see just how huge a journey Jesus made on the cross.

This was the psalm Jesus quoted when nailed to the cross. His great cry of dereliction is recorded in two of our Gospels (Matthew 27:46; Mark 15:34). This was the torment of aloneness which Jesus felt and which none of us can begin to imagine. It would have been our feelings of isolation multiplied many times over.

But on the cross, Jesus rose from that point of desolation to commit his spirit to God (Luke 23:46) and completed the work God gave him to do when he cried, 'It is finished' (John 19:30). In the Garden, amongst the Olive trees, God trusted Jesus with the plan of redemption (Matthew 26:42-44). On the cross Jesus trusted God for his salvation and ours.

A moment's meditation

> *I believe in the sun even when it is not shining.*
> *I believe in love even when I cannot feel it.*
> *I believe in God, even when he is silent.*
>
> *Written by a Jewish prisoner in Cologne.*

A personal application

The truth of the matter is that at some point in our walk with God, he leaves us with the very real impression that we are alone in our despair. In those times it is actually easier not to believe in God, for our trust in him only feeds our pain.

It's not just that God appears to have forgotten us; it's the pain of wanting to know *why* he should. What have we done wrong? In some warped way, it actually helps if we can identify horrendous sins which deserve God's anger. But when we have searched and acquitted ourselves, the pain of abandonment gets out of control. When we feel abandoned by God it ceases to be theological and becomes very personal. It is hard to trust God or anyone else.

But there is a journey of trusting faith we must all make.

First let's admit when we feel hard done by. The psalmist did, Jeremiah did (Jeremiah 20:7) and Jesus did. If Lent is a time of soul-searching, that is a very good place to start. Recognising that may be the first step in your journey of trust. If you're upset with God, he will hear you on the subject.

Then, like Jesus on the cross, you will need to move beyond the crushing feeling of aloneness to one of trust. You do this, not by working things out, but simply by committing yourself and your circumstances to his care.

And finally we make the journey of faith by being faithful in the things he has called us to do. Doing is not the issue: obedience is. Our faith is at its best not in the classroom but in the open field of responsibility and obedience. Often in the *doing* we become who we were meant to be. In showing ourselves trustworthy we often rediscover trust in God.

'It is finished' is a great statement of trusting partnership.

A prayer

Father,
   I abandon myself into your hands;
   do with me what you will.
Whatever you may do I thank you:
   I am ready for all, I accept all.

Let only your will be done in me,
    and in all your creatures.
I wish nothing more than this, O Lord.

Into your hands I commend my soul:
    I offer it to you
    with all the love of my heart,
    for I do love you, Lord,
    and so I need to give myself,
    to surrender myself into your hands,
    without reserve,
    and with boundless confidence,
    because you are my Father.

Charles de Foucauld

Talk time

- What did it mean for David and Jesus to have felt abandoned in their moment of need? Did God really forsake Jesus or did he just *feel* as though God did?

To do

- Can you identify the things around you which are most likely to undermine your trust in God? They may appear to be your cross.

- Make a list of your giftings or responsibilities. Are you fulfilling them to the best of your ability?

- Make a note of things God has given you to do which you feel you have left undone. How might you get back on track?

Week 4
Hope to Trust

> *Those who trust in the Lord are like Mount Zion,*
> *which cannot be shaken <u>but endures for ever</u>.*
>
> *As the mountains surround Jerusalem,*
> *so <u>the Lord surrounds his people</u>*
> *both <u>now and for evermore.</u>*
>
> *Psalm 125:1, 2*

Reflections from the Psalm

People under intense pressure and stress find it hard to think about the future. Talking to a family friend some years ago that became very evident. A scientist by training, she had fallen on difficult times and wandered away from God. So much had gone wrong that she was overwhelmed by her present circumstances and was struggling to trust again. She became locked into the present. After a number of meetings I attempted to get her to talk about the future. I wanted her to tell me three hopes for the future and how she planned to see them through. She couldn't do it. The future had become a foreign language.

The psalmist trusted not only because he had a God who had been faithful in the past, but also because his God gave assurances about the future. People who trust in God are like Mount Zion *now*: stable and unshakeably firm. And they are like that because they have a promise that they will endure forever. As the mountains snuggle the city of Jerusalem, so God's ring of confidence embraces the trusting ones. And God will do so for all times.

Trust is possible because God is as confident about the future as he is relaxed about the past. David knew that trust rests on the power of God's promises.

A moment's meditation

> *I said to the man who stood at the gate of the year: 'Give me*
> *a light that I may tread safely into the unknown'. And he*
> *replied: 'Go out into the darkness and put your hand into*
> *the hand of God. That shall be better than light and safer*
> *than a known way'.*

Minnie Louise Haskins

A personal application

Twenty-first century Christians live in a world of the immediate. The *now* experience governs everything from our mood swings to our legislative processes. That is partially because our senses are incessantly swept by data which demands *now* responses. Quick deals and special offers bully us into buying now. And the sheer volume and immediacy of the news plugs us into a world of *now* disasters and reactions. Tsunamis and suicide bombers come immediately to our attention, creating immediate fears and anxieties. In our shrinking world everything is nearby now.

And given that things now happen so fast, few of us dare guess what tomorrow looks like. Futurologists are treated with the same scepticism as weather forecasts. Increasingly fewer companies take 10-year strategies seriously. In our 'portfolio culture' long term is a 3-5 year stint.

In our instant world the future has become intangible and unintelligible. The pains and anxieties of our now society have much to do with the fact that so many of us have become prisoners of the suffocating present. We have been locked in on ourselves with no windows to future hope. What we see and experience has come to define who we are destined to be.

But God is a future God. This is the message of Good Friday and Easter Sunday morning. Death does not have the last word over our lives, and for people who trust in God the resurrection is merely a down-payment on a better future. Trusting in God is to trust in the God of hope; and hope is far more powerful than optimism. This trusting hope is anchored in a very simple truth: God will be here tomorrow. And if God has a future, we can trust him. If he has no future, the life we live in the now is merely an illusion and simply not worth having.

As Jesus said, 'Because I live, you will also live'.

We should not become trapped in the present. Neither our joy nor our hopes depend on today's opportunities which come knocking, for we hold them lightly. And we are never bullied by our tough conditions, even when they make us doubt.

Trusting today is possible because we have a tomorrow-God who makes us people of hope, and because we know that hope is heaven on earth.

A prayer

Lord,
    you are never captivated by the demands of the day.

We thank you that in the busyness and demands of this day,
    your love has hemmed us in
    and your grace has guided our lives.

And we thank you for the security we have in you.
You are our mountain;
    and the safe place on which we stand.

We trust you.

Protect us from the tyranny of the now.
Guard us from the things which crouch
    to overwhelm us now.

And as we rejoice in your goodness to us now,
    we thank you for the hope
    you put within us.
Motivate us with that hope.

Captivate and clothe us with that hope.
Let this hope take us from our past,
   and lead us through this present
   into your presence.

Amen.

Talk time

- How can we live in a society which emphasises the immediate so much and still think about future hope?

- If hope is much more than optimism, what is the difference between the two?

To do

- Make a note of news items this week. See how far you view them from the perspective of the future. How will this influence your attitude to people who do evil or those who suffer innocently?

Week 5
Trustees of the Kingdom

Do not put your <u>trust in princes</u>,
  in mortal men, who cannot save.
When their spirit departs, they return to the ground;
  on that very day <u>their plans come to nothing</u>.

Blessed is he whose help is the God of Jacob,
  whose <u>hope is in the Lord his God</u>,
  the Maker of heaven and earth,
  the sea, and everything in them —
  the Lord, who remains faithful for ever.
He <u>upholds the cause of the oppressed</u>
  and gives food to the hungry.
The Lord <u>sets prisoners free</u>,
  the Lord gives sight to the blind,
  the Lord <u>lifts up those who are bowed down</u>,
  the Lord loves the righteous.
The Lord <u>watches over the alien</u>
  and <u>sustains the fatherless and the widow</u>,
  but he frustrates the ways of the wicked.

The Lord reigns for ever,
  <u>your God, O Zion</u>, for all generations.

Psalm 146:3-10

Reflections from the Psalm

The Henley Research Centre did a survey some years ago of 'brands' people trusted. It turned out that the Church came eighth behind brands such as Kellogg's. The feeling was that if you opened up a packet of cornflakes you could be fairly confident about the contents, but you might not be as confident about the Church!

The psalmist – not David this time – also had a problem with leaders. His advice was very stark. Don't trust them totally! Of course this was not an anti-prince campaign. It was political common sense. For although princes have responsibilities, they too are mortal, and at the best of times their very best plans fall to the ground or leave the stage of history along with them. Of the multitude of leaders at any given time, a mere handful are likely to leave behind monuments of hope.

No, the writer insists our trust should be in the Lord whose creative power tells of his abiding faithfulness. And what is even more important, this God in whom we trust has the marginalised at heart. The oppressed, hungry and prisoner all command his attention. He watches over the foreigner, fatherless and widow.

This is good government. In the psalmist's mind there is a juxtaposition between mortal princes who rule and the sovereign God who reigns. This kingdom of fair play and justice, therefore, becomes the template by which all princes should be judged. If their work lasts, it will last because it lives up to the profile of the rule of God: a kingdom in which everyone is protected.

And if he is 'your God, O Zion' think how much Zion – the people of God – should be implicated in that kind of society! In this picture Zion must be more than recipients: Zion must become that kind of place.

A moment's meditation

> How small, of all that human hearts endure,
>   that part which laws or kings can cause or cure!
> I put my trust in thee.
>
> The Traveller, Oliver Goldsmith

A personal application

It is true that many people no longer trust the Church as much as they once did, but there's also good news. In a 2003 European Union survey 43 per cent of the people polled said they still trusted the Church and an incredible 70 per cent said they still trusted Christian leaders, compared with 54 per cent who trusted politicians.

Bashing public servants has become a popular pastime. That is not our Christian calling. Of course we all have the right to trustworthy leaders and people of influence. No one on the operating ward wants to see their surgeon walk in with a T-shirt with 'Oops! I dropped the knife!' written on it. When we put our future in other people's hands we want to know that they are trustworthy.

Having said that, perhaps in our reflections a good place to start is to acknowledge that leaders are 'princes' with limitations. To do this is a liberating step for them and for us, because it gives them the right to be wrong and it gives us the responsibility to support our leaders when they fail. In rebuilding trusting communities Christians have a responsibility to remind everyone that politicians are people too!

As trustees of the kingdom we are called to do more than lament the lack of trust. Ours is the privilege to challenge and agitate by our words and deeds for a more trusting society. And a trusted person in the home, workplace or sportsfield is an effective antidote to the cynicism which so easily destroys our communities. A trustworthy lifestyle is a powerful contribution to the restoration of our communities.

And beyond that, our devotion and commitment to the 'Maker of heaven and earth' will be to join him in the enterprise to free the world of inequality and oppression. We may give up many things this Lent, but we should never surrender the passion to work with God on this agenda.

A prayer

Lord,
    make me an instrument of your peace.
Where there is hatred let me sow love,
    where there is injury, pardon;
    where there is doubt, faith;

where there is despair, hope;
where there is darkness, light;
where there is sadness, joy.
O divine Master, grant that I may not so much seek
to be consoled as to console,
to be understood as to understand,
to be loved as to love;
for it is in giving that we receive;
it is in pardoning that we are pardoned;
it is in dying that we are born to eternal life.
Amen.

St Francis of Assisi

Talk time

- In an article in the *Times,* the Radio 4 broadcaster John Humphries wrote, 'Trust is the cement in the democratic structure. Lose it and you lose power'. If he is right, how should Christians respond to this warning?

- If we are not to trust in 'princes', how do we pray and participate in the democratic process?

To do

- Make a list of five prominent leaders in the Church and the wider society and commit to pray for them during this Lent season. Why not add to your list beyond Lent!

- Our political leaders are key influencers in rebuilding communities. Why not commit to pray for and write to your local Member of Parliament?

- If you have no links with any organisation working to protect the poor and vulnerable, why not think about joining one this Lent. You may know of several Christian ministries or wish to support a reputable non-Christian agency.